DISCERNMENT

Discernment

Theology and Practice, Communal and Personal

Ladislas Orsy, SJ

LITURGICAL PRESS
Collegeville, Minnesota
www.litpress.org

Cover design by Ann Blattner. Cover illustration by Frank Kacmarcik, Obl.S.B. Interior photos courtesy of Wikimedia Commons: page 45, Lake Jocassee, South Carolina, CC-BY-SA-2.0; page 48, drawing by George Robert Bonfield, 1835.

A First Edition entitled *Toward a Theological Evaluation of Communal Discernment* was published in the series of "Studies in the Spirituality of Jesuits," St. Louis, 1973.

A Second Edition, revised and enlarged, entitled *Probing the Spirit*, was published by Dimension Books, Denville, NJ, 1976.

1 2 3 4 5 6 7 8 9

Library of Congress Cataloging-in-Publication Data

Names: Orsy, Ladislas M., 1921– author.
Title: Discernment : theology and practice, communal and personal / Ladislas Orsy, SJ.
Other titles: Probing the spirit
Description: Collegeville, Minnesota : Liturgical Press, [2020] | "First Edition entitled Toward a Theological Evaluation of Communal Discernment was published in the series of "Studies in the Spirituality of Jesuits," St. Louis, 1973. Second Edition, revised and enlarged, entitled Probing the Spirit, was published by Dimension books, Denville, NJ, 1976"—Colophon. | Includes bibliographical references. | Summary: "A collection of insights suitable for both individual and group discernment exercises rooted in Ignatian spirituality"— Provided by publisher.
Identifiers: LCCN 2020004706 (print) | LCCN 2020004707 (ebook) | ISBN 9780814685075 (paperback) | ISBN 9780814685310 (epub) | ISBN 9780814685310 (mobi) | ISBN 9780814685310 (pdf)
Subjects: LCSH: Discernment (Christian theology) | Spirituality—Catholic Church. | Ignatius, of Loyola, Saint, 1491-1556. Exercitia spiritualia. | Spiritual exercises.
Classification: LCC BV4509.5 .O76 2020 (print) | LCC BV4509.5 (ebook) | DDC 248.3—dc23
LC record available at https://lccn.loc.gov/2020004706
LC ebook record available at https://lccn.loc.gov/2020004707

Wisdom is radiant and unfading,
and she is easily discerned by those who love her,
and is found by those who seek her.
Wisdom 6:12

Dedicated to the Memory of Saint Paul VI,
Giovanni Battista Montini,
Who discerned that Vatican Council II ought to continue
And guided the Church into the path of hope.

Contents

Acknowledgments

The author's pleasant duty is to thank his Jesuit Companions close and far, and Hans Christoffersen of Liturgical Press for encouraging this project, Dr. Josie Ryan for her precious help in editing the text, and Sarah Reardon for her manyfold assistance in bringing the work to completion.

Introduction

A Multitude of Theoretical Problems

To probe the ways of the Spirit is an adventure out of the ordinary, an enterprise that is both uplifting and humiliating.

It is an adventure out of the ordinary because it is easier to look outward than to look inward. The universe that surrounds us holds our attention with its display of movements, sounds, and colors. To find the ways of the Spirit we must turn in the opposite direction: we must enter the world of silence and mystery. Once there, we become aware of new signs of life that speak about the source of all life.

To experience inwardly even fragmentary manifestations of God's power and glory is a fascinating event for any human being; it lifts a person up beyond any expectation. It is an experience of humiliation or mortification, contrary to natural human desire. It reveals fragments of God's greatness and goodness; it bares our frailty and poverty.

Key Words for Understanding

Discernment. The linguistic roots of the word are in the Latin *discerno*; the *Oxford Latin Dictionary* translates it as "separate or divide off" and "to distinguish with mind or senses," clearly indicating that it means an activity, a process. The *Oxford English Dictionary and Thesaurus* explains the word *discern* as "perceive clearly with the mind or the senses" and as "make out by thought or by gazing, listening," that is, a particular type of activity that may consist not only in formal calculations but also in informal gazing and listening—a state of consciousness akin to passive contemplation.

Consolation. The same *Thesaurus* offers an abundance of synonyms for the verb *console*, representing a variety of shades of meaning such as "comfort, soothe, calm, assuage, solace, cheer up, reassure, relieve, hearten, cheer, gladden." For our purposes, all these sorts of "consolation" can be summarized by the traditional scholastic definition of peace: *tranquillitas in ordine*—"a quiet condition of state of affairs"—because the soul has found its rightful place before God and among his people.

Desolation. For our purposes, it should be enough to say that this means any movement or state that is opposite of consolation and destroys order.

Integrity. It is a word rarely—if ever—mentioned in writings and talks about discernment. Yet, discernment is about integrity—100 percent. It is not a logical exercise to resolve a mathematical equation; it is not a quest for a *Eureka!* moment concerning a physical puzzle; it is not an effort to invoke some spirits. In our religious context, discernment is nothing else than putting ourselves into a state of readiness to surrender to truth—or into a disposition to reach out for the good—natural or supernatural.

Theoretical Issues

In the field of theology, no question stands alone; each is linked to others as closely as the arches of a Gothic cathedral are bound together. We cannot pull one out to examine it separately. It would have no meaning outside its place; besides, its removal would endanger the whole building. The innocent question "What is community discernment?" is linked with momentous problems over which theologians have battled for centuries.

Some examples demonstrate the truth of this statement.

• We usually describe community discernment as a method of finding God's will through the movements of grace in the inner being of the participants. Such a search, however, has no theological explanation unless we face the much broader question of the relationship between *divine gifts* and *human capacities*. On the one hand, we Christians are children of light with an ability to perceive the presence of divine mysteries and to receive divine life itself; on the other hand, we are creatures with a mortal body and earthy limitations.

Can we identify God's gifts with any precision? Are we able to say what comes from our resources? If we cannot answer these questions with clarity and certainty, how can we speak about discovering God's mind and will? In sum: to know how much the community can accomplish in the process of discernment, we should have a good understanding of the relationship between God's gifts and human persons' capacity to receive them.

• This leads to the kindred question of the relationship between *God's grace* and *human freedom*. After the Dominicans and Jesuits spent centuries entrapped in a futile battle over the issue, they came to the realization that the problem was more mysterious than it appeared to either side. After all, who can tell how far the good deeds of a Christian proceed from divine initiative or how deeply they have their source in human freedom and creativity? To understand the discernment process, we should know more about the respective roles of grace and freedom.

• If we knew God's providence in all its intricacies, it would be easier to handle the practice of discernment. But we have no such knowledge. The *will of God* is a complex expression. It can mean God's positive and efficacious will: he does what he wants; "For who can resist his will?" (Rom 9:19). It can also mean his permissive will, which allows evil to operate in this universe. Of course, he does not want any evil, yet he allows his free creatures to revolt against his design: "For God has imprisoned all in disobedience so that he may be merciful to all" (Rom 11:32). Between these two meanings of the term *God's will*, there are many others. In any particular situation, positive and permissive wills may be present in different combinations. How can anyone sort them all out?

• There is the problem of interpreting the *present will* of God in relation to his *future design*. On the one side, there is the naive conception that God has a special blueprint for our lives in all details and that we can discover it and make it into the norm of our actions. On the other side, there is the simplistic belief that God leaves us fully autonomous (like machines made in a factory) and that we decide the course of our life as we wish it. In truth, our God is neither the meticulous and oppressive planner nor the distant and cool observer. He is a friend with great love who respects our freedom but also has his dreams about our future. How to bring these two aspects together in harmonious concepts? Fortunately, good Christians who know no theoretical solution to this problem bring their creativity and their faith in God's providence harmoniously to bear on their decisions and have the courage to accept responsibility for their own actions. They find harmony where savants fail in their reasoning.

• We should not fear, however, to enter into a discernment. In the Church of Corinth, Paul found *gifts and charisms among ordinary folk* who were not different from Christians of today. Therefore, a good Christian community of today must have the necessary wisdom for discernment! Especially if we judge those Corinthians by their faults as well as their graces, both of which were amply described by the apostle. Precious gifts existed in that community side by side with serious deficiencies. Problems in the field of theory indeed abound. Solutions are hard to come by, but every right question is a step toward better knowledge, even if the answer is not evident or complete.

Fortunately, the gifts of the Spirit do not depend on our abstract reflections. He gives them before we can analyze them; his gifts precede our thoughts. Nor should prayerful deliberations depend on abstract responses. While theologians are working their way toward a conceptual understanding, communities that are one in mind and heart should go on praying to find out how they should take the next step in the service of the Lord. We should never delay the praise of God and the work for his Kingdom because we are not ready with our scholarly articulations.

The Lord said, "For everyone who asks receives, and everyone who searches finds, and for everyone who knocks, the door will be opened" (Matt 7:8). *Community discernment is a way of asking, seeking, and knocking.* Its method may be different from community to community; no two discernments are equal because the discerners are not equal. God respects their diversity. The all-transcending truth is that, when the community gathers in prayer, Christ is with his disciples again. *The best fruit of any discernment will always be the recognition of the Risen Lord's presence*, as it was given to the disciples of Emmaus: "They said to each other, 'Were not our hearts burning within us while he was talking to us on the road, while he was opening the scriptures to us?' " (Luke 24:32).

* * *

The practice of discernment in the Spirit has been always present in the communities of God's people—it belongs to the Jewish-Christian tradition. Anciently, Abraham "discerned" that he had to follow a mysterious call; recently, Jorge Bergoglio "discerned" that under the name of Francis he had to accept the mandate to shepherd Christ's flock.

For this reason, whatever is presented in this book, while admittedly heavily inspired by St. Ignatius, is not meant to be literal exegesis of Ignatian texts, still less authentic interpretation of his mind. It is intended to be nothing more and nothing less than a twenty-first-century contribution to Christian "wisdom literature."

* * *

Five Questions

Each community within the Church is an organized body; it is alive when there is a dynamic interplay among the members. It must have a center where one (or several) person(s) clothed with authority stand and to whom informational data flow steadily from all directions. The task of the center is to create one mind and one heart in the community, out of the multiplicity of ideas and desires, in harmony with the aspirations of the universal Church. Such organic unity among intelligent persons cannot arise if those in authority alone decide all issues and call for unconditional and blind surrender in others. The ones who preside must respond in a spirit of service to the right and just desires of all.

With the fair amount of experience that we have, it is a good time to now raise the question more explicitly, especially from the viewpoint of theological investigation: What is communal discernment? This is the purpose of this study. For the sake of clarity and orderliness, it unfolds through five specific queries:

First, what are the *theological foundations* of communal discernment?

Second, what are the *legitimate expectations* that the discernment process can fulfill?

Third, what are the *misplaced expectations*?

Fourth, what is the relationship between *authority* and *community discernment*?

Fifth, what *practical guidelines* follow from our theological considerations?

In exploring these questions, we gather our reflections around thirty-one propositions.

First Question

What Are the Theological Foundations of Communal Discernment?

Discernment Requires Contemplative Insight

1. *The fruit of discernment in its best and purest form is the articulation of a contemplative insight into the working of God's grace in human persons.*

We say "in its best and purest form" because we have to begin there. Wholeness is the clue to the understanding of the fragments. Contemplative insight means knowledge obtained not so much by human effort and creativity as through God's gracious gift; an inspiration akin to the "intimate understanding and relish of the truth" (*el sentir y gustar de las cosas internamente*) of which St. Ignatius speaks in his *Exercises* (2). We discover such knowledge by experiencing peace, gladness, joy, and encouragement in God's presence. Such psychological signs are certainly not the logical outcome of a reasoning process. In other and more biblical terms, discernment is the recognition of God's sometimes scandalous or foolish ways, "a stumbling block to Jews and foolishness to Gentiles"

(1 Cor 1:23), through the presence of the fruits of the Spirit: "love, joy, peace, patience, kindness, generosity, faithfulness, gentleness, self-control" (Gal 5:22-23).

In this process at its best, there is an interplay between God's inspiration and human exploration. To become aware of this interplay between two poles is a fundamental requirement for the understanding and consequently for the right use of the process. There is God's hidden mystery on the one side, and there is a human person who perceives it on the other side.

No wonder that such discernment requires contemplative persons versed in finding God's presence *by instinct*. A sensitivity to the gentle movements of grace is an indispensable condition. Without it there is no wholeness in discernment.

Insight into God's Ways

2. *Discernment in its fullest religious sense is about resolving spiritual issues. To do it well the discerners need to be well qualified: they must "be wise as serpents and innocent as doves" (Matt 10:16), and, of course, they must be attuned to the Spirit.*

If discernment is a contemplative insight into God's own ways, its prime use ought to be for issues that we cannot solve in any other way, such as by empirical observation and rational reflection. Then, discernment is indeed necessary: "For my thoughts are not your thoughts, nor are your ways my ways, says the Lord. For as the heavens are higher than the earth, so are my ways higher than your ways and my thoughts than your thoughts" (Isa 55:8-9). Only God can give an insight into his own plan; only he can confirm a decision that is the fruit of an attraction by the Father: "No one can come to me unless drawn by the Father who sent me" (John 6:44).

An Early Example: The Apostolic Council of Jerusalem

3. *Discernment by a believing community (known also as "communal discernment," as distinguished from an "individual" one) is not new in the Church. A reading of Luke's report on the Apostolic Council of Jerusalem reveals its essential elements (Acts 15:1-35).*

The apostles convened the Council of Jerusalem to deal with a vital issue for the nascent Church: Were the newly baptized Gentiles bound to observe the Law of Moses, including imposition of circumcision? In other words, does salvation come through the Law and its practices, as the party of Pharisees converted to Christ contended, or given feely through the gift of faith in the Risen Christ, as Paul asserted?

The future of the Church depended on this issue. Mere reasoning and logic could not solve it. After all, did not the Messiah come to uphold and perfect the Law (Matt 5:17)? Yet, he insisted also that "the sabbath was made for humankind" (Mark 2:27) and invited all nations into the Kingdom. Among such conflicting testimonies, how could the apostles decide without the light of the Spirit? They needed to discern the plan of God.

The apostles gathered together with some elders and disciples. At the core of the group was the small group who prayed together in that upper room when the Spirit of the Lord was poured out on them. No doubt, as they met to deliberate, they were united in prayer again as only they could be.

Luke describes how they pondered the issue. Interestingly, they did not much debate the merits of the question. They spoke about the witness of the Holy Spirit who cleansed the hearts of many and worked signs and wonders among them. The party of the Pharisees turned believers, then Peter, Barnabas, and Paul, all had their turn and said their piece. There was silence in the assembly during the speeches. "The whole assembly kept silence, and listened to Barnabas and Paul as they told of all the signs and wonders that God had done through them among the Gentiles" (Acts 15:12). They listened with open minds. They were searching for wisdom.

Finally, James proposed a solution based on the words of the prophets, on the signs of the times, and on some shrewd wisdom. He opted for new ways, but not without granting some concessions to older traditions. "Therefore I have reached the decision that we should not trouble those Gentiles who are turning to God, but we should write to them to abstain only from things polluted by idols and from fornication and from whatever has been strangled and from blood" (Acts 15:19-20).

James's wisdom paved the way for a consensus. The participants formulated new rules approved by them all. It included the words that later became familiar to readers of the documents of ecumenical councils. "For it has seemed good to the Holy Spirit and to us" (15:28), *placuit Spiritui sancto et nobis*: a proclamation that this decision was not the logical conclusion of a debate but a discovery granted them by the Spirit.

The Acts report that when the letter was communicated to the Church of Antioch, "they rejoiced at the exhortation" (15:31). There was peace in the congregation. The fruits of the Spirit sealed the decision.

There is a precedent of supreme authority. We follow a path traced by the apostles. The Church has practiced "communal discernment" whenever men and women graced by God have come together and set out to search for the high thoughts and ways of the Lord that no person can know through their own efforts alone.

Later Developments: Councils and Religious Groups

4. *Throughout the history of the Church, there were outstanding examples of community discernment; the most important ones occurred in episcopal councils and synods, but they also took place in religious communities, especially at the time of their foundation.*

The community of bishops, assembled in councils, universal or particular, had to discern the meaning of God's word. They were aware that their canons, decrees, and "determinations" were more than the fruit of human calculations and conjectures: they were insights into a mystery. Because of this belief, the bishops could say with authenticity: "It has seemed good to the Holy Spirit and to us" (Acts 15:28), *placuit Spiritui sancto et nobis.*

Moreover, it is legitimate to assume that discernment was a way of life in early monastic communities, in the East and in the West. Originally, monasteries harbored fervent groups seeking to find the ways of God through prayer and penance under the leadership of the abbot. Undoubtedly, the monastic "chapter," with its prayerful atmosphere and subdued discussions, grew out of a common effort to seek and find how to follow "the Way" that was Christ. The chapter developed into a regular exercise of communal discernment.

Into this enduring tradition must be inserted the practice of communal discernment used by St. Ignatius and his first companions. They did not invent communal discernment but left records of their practice of it.

The First Fathers of the Society of Jesus

5. *The process through which St. Ignatius and his first companions arrived at the decision to form a religious community is a model of communal discernment. In his Constitutions, however, he did not make it an ordinary instrument of governance.*

The early history of the Jesuits provides an outstanding example of communal discernment. One of them recorded the process in a document known as the *Deliberatio primorum Patrum*, "Deliberation of the First Fathers."

They were well disposed to enter into a holy discernment. They had lived the *Exercises* with all its divine consolations and human desolations. Ignatius, blessed with extraordinary intellect and graces well beyond our comprehension, guided them.

They faced a single, momentous matter of divine grace and human prudence—important not only for them but also for the universal church: Should they form a permanent organic body, a religious order, in fact, a legally structured "corporation," or should they remain as they were, "companions of Jesus" but with no juridical bond? If ever an issue required discernment by the criteria of the *Exercises*, through the movements of grace-filled consolations and desolations, that was the one. They were equal to the task.

After months of prayer and discussion, these "pilgrim priests" decided to form a permanent order, and the Society of Jesus was born. History has proved their spiritual insight. They discovered a divine intent through the process of discerning the grace in their midst.

When the time came to compose Constitutions for the new order, however, Ignatius—as the formally elected superior general—did what virtually all founders had done over the span of a thousand years and gave his companions a legally binding document infused with structured procedures and with checks and balances at all levels.

Some Historical Questions about the First Jesuits

6. *To grasp the significance for our time of the events described in the early historical records of the Society of Jesus on discernment, we must interpret past events within their historical context.*

To understand what happened, we must search for the sixteenth-century meaning of the records; we should not project our own modern ideas into them. To draw practical conclusions for our times, we must go through a process of historical criticism. Any deviation from this basic rule leads to distortion of both our knowledge of history and the soundness of present practice.

Such historical reconstruction cannot, however, take place here. It would require a full-fledged study. Yet a question can and must be raised here and now to correctly make us aware of the historical dimensions of the problems. Was the *Deliberatio* "communal discernment" or was it a gentle conversion of the group to Ignatius's long cherished vision? How far did Ignatius inspire the group?

To understand the nature of this deliberation of the ten companions, we must ask to what extent the decision of the small group to form a religious order in the classical sense emerged from the group and to what extent Ignatius converted them to his own vision. Did they all, Ignatius included, begin their deliberation from the same state of ignorance, doubt, and detachment, or was one of them (Ignatius) in possession of an extraordinary vision that helped him to enlighten his companions throughout the deliberation and to raise their minds and hearts to the internal knowledge and aspiration that he possessed? If the final decision emerged fully from the group, their deliberation must be described as a truly creative process in which each played a role and played it equally, even if each contributed. If, however, Ignatius entered the process with a purpose and with a gentle and quiet assurance that God wanted him to be an instrument to enlighten his companions, then the decision originated more in one person than in many. In the first hypothesis, all would have contributed more or less equally to the process. In the second, the group would have gradually appropriated the vision of its leader.

A whole series of events in the life of Ignatius indicate an increasing desire to gather companions around himself and to form a group permanently united in the service of the Church. His painful search to find companions, marked by failures first and eminent successes later, had all the dynamics toward organizing a group that would stay together. To assume that Ignatius entered this process of deliberation in a state of blank indifference about its outcome and without an interest in permanent unity in the group is to ignore the history and the dynamics of his life after his conversion in 1521. It makes good historical sense to assume that the *Deliberatio* was not a "communal" discernment in its full sense.

In fact, Ignatius himself displayed discretion in suggesting any future discernment process. In the *Constitutions* (694–718), he gives detailed rules for the election of a general superior and for transacting business at a general congregation. In neither case is the pattern of the "deliberation" referred to, much less imposed. They are to accept a sudden and evident inspiration from the Holy Spirit for an election and may make decisions by acclamation, that is, by one common acceptance of a powerful movement of the Spirit. Ordinarily, however, they must hold elections and make decisions through the humble means of votes given and counted. Never in their history have Jesuits elected a superior general by unanimous acclamation.

St. Ignatius gives instructions in the *Exercises* for discernment by individuals. The question emerges: How should communities apply those rules to a group?

The transfer of the "Rules for the Discernment of Spirits" (*Exercises* [313–36]), conceived for individual spiritual direction, into community situations is a complex process. Each person remains unique even when he is a member of a community;

yet the community is one through a bond that transcends individual differences. Each person must be given the respect that is due to an intelligent and free child of God, yet the common mind and the common will of the group must be taken into account. Delicate balances are necessary to satisfy the demands of both sides and to bring about the desired harmony between the two. Those balances cannot be fixed by permanent and static measures; they must shift and change, bringing to the fore the uniqueness of the person at one time, the common mind and common heart at another time.

How should communities accomplish this adaptation? The answer may be easier in practice than in theory. Unless we are able to formulate guidelines based on sound theology, sooner or later some communities will be misled by a combination of goodwill and theological ignorance. If we do not achieve the right balance, either the person will suffer or the imbalance will destroy the common spirit.

All of these issues demand critical inquiry in depth, but it does not follow that while the work of historical and theological investigation goes on, communal discernment should stop. Enough valid insights have already emerged to guide wise men and women in search of progress in God's service, provided they are conscious that there is still much to learn. To reach wisdom, prudence is necessary.

Discernment in Our Days

7. *Communal discernment can be used by lesser spiritual giants than St. Ignatius and for resolving more modest issues than the founding of a new religious order, provided that from*

beginning to end the members of the discerning group are aware of their limitations.

Two principles are implied in this statement, both fairly obvious. One says that the more remote a person is from contemplative insight, the less he or she should presume that he or she is able to discover reliably the movement of grace in a community. The other tells us that we should expect no extraordinary illumination from the Spirit when the ordinary use of human intelligence assisted by grace is enough to decide an issue. That is, communal discernment will be an instrument of progress for humble folk who know their own limits. For others, it will become rapid transport into a dream world filled with illusions. Let us see more closely, therefore, what discernment about an earthly issue looks like in an ordinary community.

Such discernment is commonly understood as a method for reaching a decision through a pattern of prayerful reflections to which all contribute. The process can be complex. Its result is more than the sum of individual judgments or decisions; the fruit is produced by all. The method requires the sharing of all available data and insights into known facts, the critical examination of opinions, and finally settling on a decision. It includes even more an alertness to the movements of grace in each person throughout the whole process. There is an interplay among the members; the community thinks, speaks, and acts as an organic body where each person has a unique role to play.

The correct understanding of this "communion" in action lies between two extreme conceptions. One exalts the unity of the community to the point that respect due to persons is destroyed; the other stresses the individual differences so far that the community vanishes in the process. Both are wrong; the truth is in the middle: all human beings are persons who find their fulfillment in a community. To be a person is to have the highest dignity in this creation. Persons, intelligent and free, have a right to develop according to their own internal light and at their own pace. Ultimately all data, all information are received by individual minds; all insights that bring meaning into them are generated by the individual intelligence; all judgments that confess the truth are made personally; and all decisions for good or evil spring from personal sources. Each person remains autonomous throughout the process of communal discernment.

Yet no person exists alone; each must be integrated into a community. Integration is more than a loose association among many. Each retains their own personhood, enriched by all the others in a new unity. The information gathered by each becomes the property of all; insights into facts are shared, judgments are construed through mutual help, and, finally, options are chosen as inspired by a common ideal.

The primacy of the person must be affirmed even in a community; otherwise, the highest dignity in creation would be diminished and its gifts diffused in some kind of collectivity. In no situation should any person renounce the use of his or her own intelligence and freedom. Yet those who form a community can do much to enhance mutually the operation of the intelligence and freedom of each person, even to the point that they all reach a broader horizon and higher viewpoint and come to the same decision; that is, they become of one mind and of one heart. Such unity is all the more possible when they take as their inspiration a common source—from the Gospel as professed by the Church—and when assisted by the same mysterious strength only the Spirit of God can give.

Communal discernment can be fruitful only when respecting the integrity of each person. The community can never take away the intelligence and the freedom of its members, but it can do much to guide them to avoid false judgments and to evade wrong decisions originating in biased minds. The community can create a climate of prayer to ensure that grace and wisdom prevail over the pull of prejudices and of selfish interests. Besides, there is the mysterious action of the Spirit who can help toward a communal vision and can strengthen the group for concerted action.

Individuals who are unable to make autonomous judgments and independent decisions, those who are thrown about by every wind that blows in the community, are not fit to make a valuable contribution toward a sound judgment and a well-grounded decision since they have nothing to contribute.

It follows that communal discernment is for strong persons. They must go through a thorough preparation, reflection, and prayerful consideration, as if they had to decide the issue alone. If the majority are weak or not well prepared, the discernment may end with the disoriented leading the others into darkness. Then, there is no communal discernment but imposition by a few after whom the others drift.

No Mean Task

8. *Communal discernment about earthly affairs should be a critical process through which the community attempts to*

> *appropriate the best insight existing somewhere among the members and make it into the community's own judgment.*

The community in the process of discernment must be aware of the hard truth that no insight is deeper, no judgment is better, just because many voice it. The number or people who support an opinion is no guarantee for quality. Yet many pairs of eyes can see more than one. Those who participate in the search can pool their information and help each other in the movement that produces well-grounded judgments and decisions.

Ideally, nothing less than the best judgment should do. Communal discernment would defeat its own purpose if creative insights and well-founded judgments were watered down to a common denominator acceptable to all. It follows that the internal dynamics of such deliberations ought to be a critical process toward the most penetrating insights and the most prudent decisions that can emerge from the group. No mean task!

It is particularly essential to stress this thesis with groups of religious men and women. The history of religious communities shows how much the vision and determination of one person inspired a new movement and led many others to an intensely dedicated life that otherwise they could not have realized. It should be enough to mention such names as Benedict, Francis, Dominic, Ignatius, Teresa of Avila, John of the Cross, Francis de Sales, Vincent de Paul, Teresa of Calcutta, and so many others. There is no historical evidence to show that, without them, a large group of followers could have produced the same insight and could have shown the same determinations as these women and men did.

There is a trend today spread over many fields, from politics to religion, which seems to believe that the correctness of a judgment or the rightness of a decision depends on the numbers that make it and not on the reasons that support it. Anyone for whom history is the "teacher of life," *magistra vitae*, knows that the best insights never come easily, that well-founded judgments are a rare commodity and total dedication to a good cause is a choice gift granted to a few.

God's Light and Humanity's Weakness

9. *Ordinarily, communal discernment is a dynamic process in which the light and strength of God's Spirit and the blurred vision of humanity all play their part. In it, a sinful community forms a judgment or makes a decision in God's luminous presence. Thus, the final result is likely to be a composite of inspiration from the high and human intelligence from the low.*

In our real world, this mixture of contrasting elements is the clue to assessing the value of communal discernment. Through it the community meets with God, in a grace-filled environment, and makes a step forward in the service of the Lord. The contrasts must be there; they are manifestations both of our divine intent and our human condition. Moreover, the members of the group are at various stages of their human and Christian development. Persons do not receive the gifts of wisdom and intelligence overnight; differences in outlook, in understanding, and in maturity remain.

Such differences play their role throughout the discernment process. While we can publish information regarding data, not all participants can grasp it with the same breadth and depth. The communication of an insight is more difficult. Clues can be given, but the light that brings understanding must come from inside; it must be generated by the person's intelligence, *intellectus agens*. No one can substitute for another. Persons in thrall to prejudices must cure themselves from the inside. Disordered attachments can be broken only by liberating the spirit—again from the inside. A person can receive powerful help but, finally, he or she is the moral agent who must act.

The techniques of discernment, such as all participants focusing on one side of the issue first and on the other side second, are concerned with the right balance among various contributions in the process. Yet no technique can ever do justice to all the differences that follow from the distinction of persons. Happen what may, throughout the process, the individual must remain his or her whole self. To fall under the spell of some fascination or to become the victim of some pressure in order to avoid a discordant note is to fall into a situation all the more dangerous because it has the appearance of harmony.

The Discovery of a Gift—The Creation of a Decision

10. *In a given case, the proper expectation of the discerners may be either a light as a gift of grace or a well-grounded judgment as produced by critical intelligence—or a combination of both.*

There is a difference between a knowledge that only God can give (since it transcends our capacity even in our graced condition) and a knowledge that we can reach (since it is within the capacity of our own intelligence healed and strengthened by God's grace). Some examples will help to make this distinction clear.

No amount of reasoning by the apostles and elders could have led them to an absolute certainty about the dispensation from Jewish laws for converts from paganism; the leaders of the fledgling Church needed an assurance from the Spirit. Once they received that gift from above, they had to rely on the capacity of their intelligence in order to make many decisions about developing organizational and operational issues of concern.

If the following of evangelical counsels is a gift from God, no one but the Holy Spirit can call a person to such a way of life or can inspire a group to form a new religious order. The light that leads into such a new state of life must be *discovered.* The discernment process ought to be, in that case, a path to discovery.

The members of a community already constituted may begin plans for the opening of a new school. They need to consider many things: the good of the students, of the parents, and of a particular parish. By using their natural intelligence infused by grace, they should be able to decide for themselves. To expect the Spirit to intervene by a singular act of revelation (e.g., should the school be coeducational or not?) would be to tempt God. From their own resources of prudence and common sense, the community should be able to make a choice.

Another image may help us further clarify the distinction. When the object of discernment is a new light that a human mind can only receive, such a person must prostrate before God in fasting and prayer, ready to learn from above what he or she cannot know by himself or herself (e.g., whether one has a vocation to be a monk or nun). When the object of discernment is a decision about human things, however, the right course of action is to use all available human resources toward a sensible outcome.

The line between a pure gift from God and a product of human intelligence must not be blurred. It gives the clue to the understanding of the call of Abram, of Moses, and of so many other prophets in the Old Testament. It makes it possible to explain, without diluting them, the words of Jesus to the apostles, "You did not choose me but I chose you" (John 15:16). A strong conviction has always existed in the Church that Francis of Assisi received a specific mission from God that no amount of meditation and reflection could have revealed to him: "Build my church." A pure gift.

This distinction is of fundamental importance because the nature of an issue must determine the approach. In the case of a divine gift, it should be humble petition and waiting for God's own time to reveal his thoughts, as Ignatius so wisely directs in the matter of election in the *Exercises*:

> While one is engaged in the Spiritual Exercises, it is more suitable and much better that the Creator and Lord in person communicate himself to the devout soul in quest of the divine will, that he inflame it with his love and praise, and dispose it

> for the way in which it could better serve God in the future. (*Exercises*, 15)

In the case of a human product, we must compose a decision with the ordinary gifts of nature and grace, knowing that, whatever the decision is, God will not fail to stand by his children *even to the point of bringing good out of our mistakes.*

Second Question

What Are the Legitimate Expectations from Communal Discernment?

To determine the legitimate expectations from communal discernment, two further questions must be raised: (1) What can a community intent on discernment expect from the Lord? and (2) What can the community achieve by its own effort?

The first question points out that there are gifts that no human being can conquer by force; they are given only through the goodness of the Lord. The second implies that there are decisions that a Christian, enlightened by faith, strengthened by hope, and prompted by love, can make.

The Presence of the Risen Lord

11. *Above all, whenever a community convenes to discern, they should be aware of the promise of the Lord: "For where two or three are gathered in my name, I am there among them"*

> *(Matt 18:20). The gathering itself signals and brings about divine presence; it creates a sacramental environment.*

It is legitimate to expect the active presence of the Lord among those who come together in his name. He himself promised it: "Again, truly I tell you, if two of you agree on earth about anything you ask, it will be done for you by my Father in heaven. For where two or three are gathered in my name, I am there among them" (Matt 18:19-20). The success of this prayer, of course, presupposes a community that lives by faith, hope, and love, not ruled by uncontrolled passion.

When the community comes together, the Lord is with it. His presence is dynamic, that is, purifying and intent on a mission for the sake of his Kingdom.

The presence of the Lord is quiet and strong. It does not work wonders and miracles overnight, but it gives wisdom and strength to the members. We need not feel it in our senses but must understand that "Jesus is Lord."

In fact, to come together for community discernment can lead to a new awareness of the Lord. Prayerful concentration on seeking his will may not bring a precise answer to a question determined by the community, but it strengthens our will to serve him. It is a redeeming presence; a far greater gift than a particular answer to a particular problem could be.

When we consider that the future of a religious community may well depend on its contemplative depths, a newly found, collective awareness of the Lord's presence may be the beginning of a new lease on life.

The Grace of Healing

12. *The dialectics of prayer and reflection may lead to the discovery of new graces, even unexpectedly, and, in any case, it has a healing effect on the community.*

Indeed, when all in the community shed their preoccupations and focus on seeking and finding God's will, this creates a convergence of intentions and initiates a movement in a common direction, which is a liberation from private and selfish projects. It is a significant step toward creating a unity of minds and hearts.

When prayer and reflection come together, we affirm and restore the integrity of our nature. Through grace, our being is rooted in God; through intelligent reflection, our humanity develops. We become whole. We cannot have a better preparation toward a wise decision. Even the object of the inquiry may become secondary when with joy we discover a new equilibrium in our being and in our gathering.

The results may surprise us. We may find that God had new insights and fresh purposes in store for us. Such an event, however, is exceptional. Our expectation should be modest: God present in the discovery of the ordinary rhythm of our lives.

Increased Prudence and Wisdom in a Community

13. *The sharing of the knowledge of disturbing facts, of prudent evaluations of critical events, of sound and generous proposals for the future are bound to benefit all and raise them to a higher level of understanding.*

A well-managed communal discernment process can bring intense development of a common vision and unity of purpose, provided each person partaking in it is ready to give what he or she has and is ready to accept what others offer. Through such exchanges, each has the opportunity to be lifted up to higher viewpoints and to more penetrating intelligence. For each and all, discernment becomes a process of enrichment and liberation.

Discernment in community should be a process of building and of liberation. The available information needs critical examination to become worthy evidence. We must discard unsubstantiated facts and complete incomplete data. Insights must come from many directions, and the community must adjust them to the facts with utmost precision; otherwise, they lead to fantasies. They must trim some insights because they go beyond the evidence and extend others since they do not take into account all the evidence. Eventually the community must come to grips with reality by making a firm judgment on the validity of an option; this is how we build unity of minds and hearts. Each must make his own contribution; each must be restrained enough to let others contribute too. It means building with precision, progressing continually in finding the right measure between two extremes: underachieving and overreaching.

To underachieve means to overlook present complexity and to ignore future consequences. It is an escape from whole truth and is therefore disastrous. To overreach is to construe more than is warranted by the evidence and is another way of betraying the truth. Theories that go beyond the evidence lead the community into a world of fantasy. No one will be able to stay there for long; dream castles are doomed to collapse. Danger may come from participants who are either "committed optimists" or "dedicated pessimists." The former tend to look only at the bright side of the problem; the latter take notice only of its dark side. They do not want to surrender to the truth as it is or to face the liberating wholeness of the given reality; they prefer an artificial construct. This is a sort of captivity of the mind.

Prayerful deliberation is a liberation process. Each person helps the others progress from ignorance to the perception of facts, from prejudices to better judgments, from hesitation to decisions. Ascent to wisdom is also ascent to freedom.

Such liberating activity, even when focused on one issue, ordinarily requires far more than the honest and prayerful consideration of the arguments only in favor of or only against a course of action. Dialectical consideration of the opposites can certainly be of help, especially at the beginning, but it also needs active input. When building a house, the strength and beauty of the construction come from the cooperation of all: the architects, engineers, decorators, and others. Similarly, the building of a wise decision requires the careful pooling of all appropriate resources.

The Quality of the Fruit Depends on the Quality of the Tree

14. *The potentials of a person or of a group are fair indications as to how far they are likely to progress through discernment.*

The potentials of a person or of a community are limited. As a tree cannot bear fruit beyond its capacity, so a human person cannot exceed the capacity of their grace and nature. The potential of a group, too, is always limited, notwithstanding the presence of the Risen Lord. The most they can hope for is that the members will reach the best judgment and the wisest decision within their capacity. Such fruit requires the conversion of the whole community to the best insight and desire found in the group—not an easy achievement! All need to grow slowly toward deeper insights and more prudent options. That is the problem! Massive group conversions happen rarely, and no one should attempt to force them.

It would, however, be too much to expect that in the course of communal discernment the best judgment will always prevail. Our salvation history shows abundantly that when prophets proclaim a message from God, they often remain a voice crying in the desert. The community is slow to grasp their message and is at times hostile to it. True prophets are never self-appointed and are mostly lonely people, appreciated more by posterity than by contemporaries. It follows that the legitimate expectation as the fruit of a communal discernment is rarely the emergence of what is best in the group but rather the standard that the majority of the members can reach and grasp. A modest accomplishment, maybe, but a real one. We should not be disappointed. If we watch a group of runners, it is not realistic to expect that all will keep up with the fastest one and reach the goal at the same time; the group's achievement will be less than that. If they all want to keep together, the fastest runner must slow down. In that case, their common achievement will not be a record speed but rather arriving together, remaining close to one another.

Admittedly, such material analogy does not do justice to a spiritual situation. Nonetheless, it helps us understand one precise point: it is unreasonable to expect that the objectively right but complex judgments and objectively prudent but hard decisions will always gather consensus. Many in the community may not have the capacity or the disposition to understand the complexity of the problem or may not have the strength to face a necessary harsh option. Indeed, God may not want them to do so here and now. He is the God of patience and forbearance. His pedagogy throughout the time of the Old and New Covenants has been to introduce his people step-by-step into the fullness of truth and love.

To sum it up, judgments and decisions at the end of communal discernment will display human limitations.

This is not to deny the reality and the value of Christ's presence. In spite of the community's inherent limitations, it is effective. It brings light and strength to the community, but in the Lord's own way. It helps the pilgrims to progress on the road, but it does not imply a promise that at no time will they make a false step.

We do not know with precision how the Lord's presence operates, but we do know by faith that it brings a mysterious and mighty help to those who are gathered in his name.

One Step Forward in the Service of the Lord

15. *The best measured expectation is that through discernment the community will take a step forward in the service of the Lord.*

A Christian community is God's pilgrim people. He leads them by twists and turns toward the Promised Land. Their pilgrimage may include events analogous to those recounted in the Bible: the flight from Egypt, the hurried wading through the Sea of Reeds, the confused and seemingly aimless wandering in the desert, the perilous conquest of their new home against fierce resistance, and, finally, the daily work of sowing seeds, planting vineyards, threshing wheat, and treading grapes. Our modern pilgrimage, no less than the old, is a journey into the unknown among many uncertainties. It requires much patience! God has his own ways and no one can force his hand. Communal discernment is not meant to lay the future bare. Christ made no such promise to his disciples.

Rather, he stressed that the life of those whom he sends to proclaim the Good News will be full of uncertainties. They must be prepared to be as defenseless as sheep are among wolves. Even if some good people will open their house and offer them hospitality, others will not. They may be insulted, attacked, and expelled from the locality; their life may be in jeopardy. Throughout their perilous journey, they will not be able to see the future laid out for them. The assurance given to them promises no less and no more than God's ongoing care and protection.

Community discernment, then, is not a means to detect the future. It has a different purpose: it helps the community to become aware of the next step and gives them the strength to take it—be it through the desert, in the battle, or in carrying out the mandate of bringing the good news to all people. We can correctly describe finding the next step, limited as it is, as discovering the will of God.

"Will of God"—What Does It Mean?

16. The expression "will of God" carries many meanings, numerous enough to trap the unwary.

An attempt to analyze what "will of God" means immediately recalls subtle distinctions between God's positive will and his permissive will. It recalls also bitter disputes between Dominicans and Jesuits who locked themselves for so long into the wrong question about divine initiative and human freedom. Past animosities should caution us of the danger of falling again into a similar trap. Many holy persons did not have or need a scientifically elaborate concept to seek and to find God's will. Their progress did not depend on sophisticated theology.

Nonetheless, some pitfalls should be known; after all, we do not have the sure instinct of saints. Therefore, some clarification of the idea of "God's will" is necessary.

One mistake would be to assume that we have to discover a precise plan, a blueprint drawn up by God for every move in our life. No, his providence does not work in that way. The details of a plan somehow emerge out of our own resources of nature and grace. God seals them by making all events work to the good of those who love him. "We know that all things work together for good for those who love God, who are called according to his purpose" (Rom 8:28).

Another mistake would be to assume that God has no plan for us at all. He would be like a father who, once his children reach adulthood, tells them, "Go your own way; I have nothing to say. You will have to make your own life." Such analogy is mistaken. God is a good parent who, throughout our life, has a plan for us. He reveals it gradually, calls us to follow it through gentle inspirations and hard awakenings, through all that ever happens to us internally and externally.

Between those two extremes we must find our way. At one time, we must create a decision after grace-filled and intelligent deliberations. At another, we have to wait for light and strength that we cannot command by ourselves. Granted, there is something new in either case. In one case, however, the fruit comes of the ordinary potentials of the tree; in the other, God's intervention produces the fruit that the tree could not bear.

To conclude, it is legitimate to expect that through discernment the community finds God's will, provided it is understood that in the pragmatic order this means simply the next step by a group of pilgrims in the service of the Lord.

Third Question

What Is It That the Community Should Not Expect?

Respect for God's Freedom

17. No community has a right to tempt God by trying to force him to grant them some extraordinary gift (e.g., private revelation, mandate of prophecy, etc.). Such an attempt would border on practicing magic.

If the dynamics of the discernment are toward the discovery of a grace that God offers to the community, there must be some previous inspiration from God to put them on that search. The instruction we received from the Lord for prayer applies to discernment too: "Very truly, I tell you, if you ask anything of the Father in my name, he will give it to you. Until now you have not asked for anything in my name. Ask and you will receive, so that your joy may be complete" (John 16:23-24). Such prayer is powerful even beyond the one that can move a mountain, since in all cases it brings a response from the Father of all. The interpreters of the Scripture agree that the Spirit of the Lord must inspire such a prayer of petition in the first place; otherwise, the promise does not hold. It must be a prayer for the coming of God's eschatological Kingdom, his reign in the hearts of all persons.

Discernment is, after all, a form of prayer, a question transfigured through grace into a petition. We can expect a response of the Father if the question comes from the Spirit. Then the inspiration of the Spirit and the response of the Father are two distinct moments of God's continuous care for his people.

It follows that the members of a community intent on discernment must unite deeply with Christ, not only to find an answer to their problem, but also to ask the right question in the first place. This applies especially when the community is moved to discover a new gift that is virtually equivalent to an extraordinary inspiration, as it was in the case of the first Jesuits who deliberated about founding a new religious order. God guided them toward the formulation of the right question from early times, when they first experienced the call of the eternal King; later, when they enjoyed the consolations of their fraternal union; and, finally, when he inspired them to offer themselves to the pope, so that he might send them anywhere in the world in service of the Gospel.

Even when the process of discernment is intended to lead not to a revelation that can come only from God but rather to the creation of an intelligent decision out of ordinary Christian resources, the question must be formulated with as much wisdom as is expected to be in the decision. The wrong question, especially when put in the clear-cut dialectics that allows only for an answer of yes or no, can lock the community into an endless and fruitless search. Worse still, ordinary consolations and desolations may be associated with the wrong question and then taken as signs from God to confirm the community actually moving in a wrong direction. It follows that every community discernment should begin by critically evaluating the initial question.

God Comes at His Own Time

18. *To allow enough time for deliberations is a matter of prudence; to set a date for concluding them may be a matter of wise foresight.*

"The wind blows where it wills, and you hear the sound of it, but you do not know whence it comes or whither it goes; so it is with everyone who is born of the Spirit" (John 3:8, RSV). Life processes do not tolerate a rigid framework. If they are strong and moving, they destroy artificial limits; if they are weak and tender, the limits destroy them. Whether we intend to discover the delicate movements of grace through the interplay of the members of a community or we want to come to a creative decision, it is no more realistic to set a precise date for results than to fix the day in advance for the perfect fruit of the tree. This is not to suggest that the process should be stretched out without limits; it is to say that due respect should be given to the slow work of nature and grace. A good vintner knows how to wait for the sun and the rain and how to determine the best time to pick the grapes.

A further qualification is necessary. When the Spirit moves the community toward asking God to reveal to its members what they cannot know ordinarily, they are not in a position to impose a limit or deadline on the Spirit's mysterious ways by setting a date by which he must speak.

When it is clear, however, that the answer to the question must arise from the ordinary resources of the community, it may be wise to set a tentative date by which the deliberations must close—provided that such a limit does not interfere with the life process. This is not an idle remark; we have seen many times how the temptation to reach a decision can interfere with the quiet play of living forces. The temptation is sometimes strong to put pressure on the group to produce proposals by a given time. To avoid embarrassment and ill feeling they will do so. The resulting decision will attract praise for efficiency, but there will not be much internal goodness in it. The relief and euphoria such a process brings will be followed duly by the bitter taste of the immature fruit. It may be wise to set a date tentatively; it may be even wiser to cancel it.

No Lasting Success Comes from a Forced Conversion

19. *The conversion of an individual person, as well as that of a community, cannot be produced at will.*

Every community discernment is a conversion process since it is a movement to the better understanding of the Good News and to a more radical following of Christ. Such change requires renewed vision and determination. Individuals, as well as a community, need time to broaden their horizon and even more time to adjust themselves practically to the new landscape. No one can force such newness on anyone according to an arbitrary timetable; each must assimilate it inwardly at one's own pace. More often than not, we must wait patiently while a conversion progresses.

Since in a discernment process each member of the community is helping all the others, all should be aware that to promote or to assist the conversion of another is a difficult art.

First, all who take part must become aware of their own need for conversion. A feeling of self-righteousness excludes all progress.

Then each should recall that strong differences of opinion on a given issue usually originate in different points of departure. When this happens, to begin immediately a debate for or against a motion is a waste of time, since the differences on that level have their source in differences of foundational principles, be they theological, philosophical, or psychological. The community should rather reflect on the sources of various opinions and see if they can achieve any mutual understanding and respect at that deep level. At times, persons or groups have to retrace their intellectual views and moral decisions to the original starting points. This means that individuals may have to do significant work toward dismantling their particular convictions before the community can build something together.

Eventually, when they achieve a unity or some mutual understanding about their basic assumptions, the community should face the issue that needs discernment.

At times, the proper fruit of discernment in religious communities should be in simply discarding the issue under consideration, coupled with a decision to dig much deeper and to discover the different foundations on which the mental and moral outlook of each person is built. When the participants know each other's starting point better, they may be able to construe new questions in a spirit of mutual understanding.

Intelligence Plays a Role

20. *Communal discernment is no substitute for critical intelligence.*

Critically trained intelligence is an indispensable instrument to buttress spiritual discernment.

Spiritual simplicity can lead far in the city of God, but when the issue concerns human affairs, we must bring human prudence to bear on the problem: it must serve as an indispensable framework in which spiritual intuition operates. No less a contemplative than St. John of the Cross warns repeatedly that we should glorify God by the full use of natural faculties before we ask for supernatural enlightenment. God gave us intelligence to use and we should use it fully.

Let us stress this point because an anti-intellectual disposition may easily mislead the discerners.

Christian wholeness does not consist in bypassing the intelligence in pursuit of holiness but rather in a healthy integration of our humanity with God's grace. Especially when the subject matter of discernment is partly sacred and partly secular, our intelligence has to play a role and work as far as it can go. Wanting to be "spiritual" beyond measure can harm the community by playing down the role of intelligent inquiries. God is pleased with the proper use of his creation.

The more highly trained the human intelligence is, the more it glorifies God and serves the cause of spirituality. To train the mind means principally two things: first, to enlarge its horizons, that is, to broaden the field of its vision and operation; second, to discipline it to the point where understanding and judgments are grounded in the facts available but never go beyond them.

The broadening of the horizon is a movement from childhood into adulthood, from naive simplicity into wise sagacity. Children are not able to place an issue in a broader context, for the simple reason that they do not yet have an ordered knowledge of themselves and the world around them. Since they do not have many points of reference in their memory, they tend to focus on only one or two aspects of a complex issue. Then they judge—lucidly and one-sidedly.

The expansion of horizon is, of course, not instantly complete on the threshold of adulthood; it must go on throughout our life. Often, the success of discernment depends on the vastness of the field on which the mind is able to operate. Only God knows how much harm persons who prayed deeply but thought shallowly and acted one-sidedly have done to the Church. God does not work miracles to correct our mistakes. Spiritual intuition should go hand in hand with trained intelligence.

Discipline of mind means fidelity to facts and to the rules of sound logic on the way to conclusions and decisions. Therefore, the solid foundation for communal discernment is in knowing how to assess facts precisely and to examine arguments critically. All participants must do their homework on the issue at hand. All must assimilate the problem personally and struggle with it. They must not consent to a decision unless they know the data and have a thorough grasp of the problem. The communal presupposes the personal in the process of reflection. Each must retain his integrity, his faithfulness to the vision he can achieve, his commitment to the decision warranted by the circumstances.

Criteria for Truth

21. *Consolations, while important as signals, are not necessarily guarantees of truths and prudence in the outcome.*

Consolations are signs of the disposition of a person before God. Since they are signs, and not reality itself, it is never easy to interpret them. St. Ignatius in his "Rules for the Discernment of Spirits" (*Exercises*, 313–36) gives elaborate norms to help us to construe the meaning of "experiencing consolations," yet he cautions us that deceptions or mistakes are possible in the course of interpretation.

The basic principle of these "Rules" of St. Ignatius is akin to the teaching of St. Thomas Aquinas on the knowledge of God and of things divine by affinity. Aquinas remarks that someone may come to a good understanding of Christian morality through sensing with the help of the gifts of the Spirit what is right and what is wrong, without ever having studied it conceptually. Ignatius affirms that persons who have grown in grace and wisdom respond positively to movements of the good Spirit through experiencing peace, joy, courage, and so forth and that they respond negatively to movements that come from the evil spirit by feeling restless, sad, depressed, and so on (see the "Rules for the Second Week," 328–36). Quite logically, those who follow evil will have the opposite reactions. They will respond to evil pleasures with content and elation (see the "Rules for the First Week," 312–27).

Such rules are no more than an application of the Lord's assertion that the sheep follow the good shepherd, for they know his voice (cf. John 10:4). There is a continuity from the doctrine of John on the voice of the shepherd to that of St. Thomas on affinity and finally to St. Ignatius's "Rules for the Discernment of Spirits."

Consolations or desolations may be of help in recognizing a divine inspiration. Indeed, St. Paul affirms that the experience of the Spirit leads to the knowledge of truth: "Now we have received not the spirit of the world, but the Spirit that is from God, so that we may understand the gifts bestowed on us by God. And we speak of these things in words not taught by human wisdom but taught by the Spirit, interpreting spiritual things to those who are spiritual" (1 Cor 2:12-13).

In human affairs, however, the proper criterion of truth is compelling evidence. We have it when we know that all steps have been taken to find the facts and to make the answer fit the facts. We have it when the answer covers all possible queries arising from the problem. Then we surrender to the truth.

If we lose sight of this human process, it becomes impossible to reexamine the outcome of a communal discernment that involves judgments about human affairs. The criterion of truth would be in various spiritual impressions and not in checking the evidence. Such spirituality disregards God's ordinary creation and the reality of the incarnation, and, hence, it is suspect. It follows that for a happy outcome of discernment, when it concerns human affairs, it is important to call on our critical intelligence.

The discerners—while debating—should also be aware that the judgments of the participants are not of equal value. Each moves within the limits of his or her own horizon, one narrow, another broad. One remains within a tangible and material universe; the other explores the depths of the human spirit. Yet, each may report joy, peace, and courage, even if one's judgment is incorrect.

Similar considerations apply to every practical decision and option. None of us is totally free from attachment and bias. The extent of our freedom enlarges or restricts our field of choice. We must critically evaluate every choice. Intellectual probity is a good disposition for the Spirit to build on!

Even if the whole community reports peace, joy, and courage at the end of the discerning process, some caution may still be necessary. The agreed-upon outcome may still be vitiated by common narrowness of minds or by unconscious attachments of the heart. Not even uniform contentment absolutely guarantees truth infallibly found or prudence unfailingly embraced.

The Value of Enthusiasm

22. *Enthusiasm can be a friendly driving force when it springs from an idea well-grounded critically, but it may lead to disaster when it is not disciplined by rational examination of ideas.*

This particular rule is no more than an application of an old saying among philosophers that has found its way into the *Exercises* of St. Ignatius: "From an entirely good cause, nothing but good follows, but the smallest defect is enough to produce an ill effect." Also he writes, "We must carefully watch the movement of our thought; if its beginning, continuation and conclusion is entirely good, intending nothing but good, a good angel must be the source of inspiration" (*Exercises*, 333).

There will be nothing but goodness in the actions of a person if there is a harmonious blend between the emotions from which enthusiasm springs and the mind that is capable of cool observation and critical evaluation of such movements. If there is no internal unity in a person and warm enthusiasm runs independently from a cool mind, the result will be fragmentation. If there is only cold calculation in a person but not the warmth of emotions, he or she will be as inhuman as a computer.

A community in deliberation should keep these cautionary remarks in mind. If the group is not involved in the nitty-gritty or the harsh reality of the application of beautiful ideas, they can be easily swayed by enthusiasm and consider anything that looks good and beautiful as immediately suitable for our frail and imperfect world.

Infallibility and Fallibility

23. *The discerners are fallible. Hence, the outcome of every discernment process is fallible.*

Since the Second Vatican Council, a shift has taken place in the Catholic Church. The understanding of the infallibility "with which the Divine Redeemer willed his Church to be endowed" (Denzinger, 43rd ed., 3074), as manifested through the acts of the popes and of the bishops, underwent some purification; it is interpreted in a more balanced way. During the same years, however, a new myth began to grow up that seemed to grant infallibility to persons and communities to a degree not granted to the pope or the college of bishops. It cannot be both ways. We rightly welcome a restraint on the part of the hierarchical church in its reliance on the charism of infallibility. Therefore, we rightly should restrain ourselves in presuming that groups and individuals in the church can operate infallibly.

The simple truth is that virtually any process of discernment by communities or individual persons takes place in the context of fallibility—apart, of course, from a solemn doctrinal declaration by an ecumenical council or by the pope, a rare event.

When God stirs human beings, they experience divine inspiration at a depth that is beyond our images and concepts, but, to be intelligible, it cannot stay there. The intuitive perception must be articulated in a human tongue. At times, the proclamation comes confused and obscure, as in the case of the "glossolalia" mentioned by St. Paul (1 Cor 14:1-19). If the recipient wishes to communicate, however, it should be articulate and intelligible through words and concepts that carry a meaning for others; it should be in the form of "prophecy," as Paul called it. Through such "prophecy," a mysterious movement initiated by the Spirit enters our own limited world, our culture, and our history; the ineffable takes on a human form. Persons who received such inspiration must "translate" it out of their own mental resources; they must interpret the movement of grace with everyday words. The result is that side by side with divine wisdom there will be human speech. The ineffable at the depth of the person and its articulation in human words must be welded into a unity. God's clarity and human fallibility are there together.

It follows that no person and no community can claim that they articulate the movement of the Spirit in its purity. The most they can do is to proclaim their conviction that they believe the Spirit prompted them and that they have reached the best interpretation they could give to what was intuitive and ineffable. The biblical story of Jonah, who received a genuine mandate from God but interpreted it in his own way, should be a salutary warning to all discerners. Jonah obeyed the call and announced, as instructed, that in forty days God would destroy Nineveh. The horizon of his mind was too narrow, however, to understand that God could repent of the evil he had said he would do to the people of Nineveh. When God did not do that evil, Jonah became angry. The story ends beautifully by describing how through parables and signs God helped Jonah understand that God can change his mind and his mercy can extend even to the 120,000 heathens of Nineveh.

The Spirit of God present in the Church guarantees that the message given to humanity through Jesus Christ will never be lost and that God's people will find their way to the Kingdom. Surrounded and protected by this exceptional certainty, Christians must now live within their fallibility.

To understand and accept our fallible condition leads to liberation. No one needs to pretend that he or she is a messenger of God's own revelation. Rather, all must submit their insights to the good sense of the community and ultimately to those who have the final authority to judge, namely, the pope with the college of bishops, so that what is missing in one's vision could be assessed by the ministry of the Church. Dialogue is possible in the Church precisely because we are fallible.

God never promised that each of us, or every religious group, would have the power to state the truth infallibly, but "we know that all things work together for good for those who love God, who are called according to his purpose" (Rom

8:28). A surprisingly generous blank check: God takes care of our well-meant mistakes.

The Habit of Prayer Is Necessary

24. *Prayerful reflection during communal discernment will not supplement for the lack of long years of devotion and purification.*

A habitually prayerful person will discern better in a short time than a dissipated person suddenly focusing on the issue. An analogy illuminates this: a learned and experienced surgeon will operate better and faster on the patient than a medical student who is consulting the best authorities during the operation. Improvised acts cannot take the place of a habitual skill built up over a long period. Discernment at its deepest level supposes the habit of contemplation that cannot be acquired over a few weekend workshops, intense as they may be. This principle applies as much to persons as to communities. It is of some importance that discernment should be made in a prayerful environment; it is of greater importance that those who discern should be prayerful persons. It follows that for some communities the right question is not how to discern an issue but how to create a habit of prayer, before undertaking any discernment. In other words, improvised discernment is not the way to reliable judgment.

Consensus Need Not Be the Goal: Authentic Discernment Can Allow Dissent

25. *If consensus can be reached, praised be God; if not, let us recall that to disagree is Catholic.*

Consensus is a fascinating idea. What is more beautiful than the whole community being of one mind and of one heart in the Spirit and agreeing to the same judgment that eventually leads to a common course of action? There are times when God gives such unity. The first fathers of the Society of Jesus reached it at the end of their *Deliberatio* about founding a religious order. In a different field, the laws for papal election admit the possibility of choosing a new pope by common acclamation under the inspiration of the Spirit. Consensus is certainly possible. When it is present, we have to acknowledge it, respect it, and rejoice in it.

Consensus grounded in identical opinions, however, is (and should be) a rare occurrence. Although God created everyone equal, he did not give the same gifts of nature and grace to each person. Neither did he create them exactly at the same spot in time and space; nor did he impose on them a uniform pace in their progress toward human and Christian maturity. Hence, in the practical order, rare will be the case when all come to the same conclusion through personal struggle. The overriding rule is that no violence should be done to the intelligence and to the freedom of anyone. Rather, we should anticipate different judgments and various proposals for action.

It follows that at the end of a community discernment process it is reasonable to expect a diversity of opinions. Consensus of judgment can be a gift from God, but it can be a human-made fallacy too. When it comes from above, it builds the community; when forced on each and all, it destroys the community.

There can be another type of convergence in the group. It is not in a common assent to the truth of the matter but a common experience of peace in relation to the proposed solution of a problem. Intellectually some may not approve of the answer; they may feel compelled to oppose it. They are ready, nonetheless, to accept it as the only possible one in their community, as the only one that can unify the community. A complex situation! Some minds do not find rest in the truth because they did not find the truth, but all may feel "consoled" because the result appears as the next feasible step in the service of the Lord. Such convergence is legitimate but by its very nature is fragile. Truth is not negotiable. Therefore, those who are convinced that a judgment is false or a decision is incorrect must wait for a better opportunity to move the question again.

In general, it is wiser not to extol the importance of consensus but rather to insist that those who live in a community must carry one another's burden. This burden includes less than perfect judgments, less than the best course of action. The bond of a community was never in identical judgments, but they accepted a conclusion for the sake of charity that may cover a multitude of differences. To find perfection in charity means to accept the wisdom of a legitimate majority, or at times to accept their lack of wisdom. We have to find peace not so much in perfection as in accepting an imperfect world.

The Paradox of Peaceful Mistakes

26. *To assess the value of the outcome of a community discernment process, we must keep in mind that the subjective experience of peace and joy in the Lord is compatible with objectively misplaced judgments and wrong decisions.*

This statement should not come as a surprise any more. It simply sums up much of what we have seen before: that a discerning community cannot be infallible or indefectible in any kind of process. Consequently, sincere efforts of its members to reach the objective truth or choose the correct option may fail, but such a limitation does not make them less acceptable to God. Provided their intentions are pure and good, God loves them and guides them through their struggling and imperfect humanity.

God never wants more from a human person than the step that they can take here and now. Once a person or a community takes that step, God is pleased and leaves the conscience of his servants at peace.

Where do we go from here?

Keeping in mind the paradox, we can arrive at a better understanding of the meaning of such signs as peace, joy, and the like in the discernment process. They are indicators of the relationship of a person or of a community to God. They are not proofs that a given judgment or decision conforms to the objective order of things or is the wisest one. No wonder, since those dispositions are ultimately the signs of a good conscience, and conscience concerns our relationship to God.

Once we understand this paradoxical situation, it becomes clear that there are no shortcuts through the laws of nature. The criterion for truth is in objective evidence, followed by the assent of the mind to a judgment. This process by the intelligence cannot be left out or watered down without penalty, not even in a discernment process. God made this world as it is; this is what philosophers call the objective world. We must conform to God's intent if we want to give glory to God.

It follows also that we should use the expression "finding the will of God" with caution. As we indicated earlier, it would take volumes to explicate the complexities of the will of God as we can comprehend it. Yet for practical purposes, we can make a useful distinction. At a given moment for us, the will of God is that we should do our best to progress toward him, that we should try to take the next step in his service, even if that step, unknown to us, may be objectively mistaken. For God, the interior disposition matters, but God also created the world outside us with its laws independent from us. If the action of a person does not conform to that pattern, no matter how well someone means, disorder may ensue. Human beings will suffer, and institutions will pay the price.

It does not follow that discernment should not be used. It follows only that we should know that its greatest value is to reaffirm our relationship to God. It is not meant to bring extraordinary revelations. Once the group is aware of such a limitation, they are well disposed to use the precious instrument they have in hand.

It follows that, once the discernment process concludes, its results should not be presented with the words of the Acts of the Apostles and ecumenical councils: *placuit Spiritui Sancto et nobis*, "it pleased us and the Holy Spirit." Rather, the community should praise God and trust that he will never let it be separated from Jesus Christ. Nothing else matters.

Fourth Question

What Is the Relationship between Authority and Discernment; What Is the Role of Discernment in a Community under Legitimate and Active Authority?

By its very nature, the purpose of community discernment is to find inspiration for action; the purpose of external authority is to create order in the group. The two sources of sustenance, the one spiritual the other legal, must complete and balance each other for the overall benefit of the social body. In our sacred time of having been redeemed, they must do it in an environment transfused by grace. Never otherwise.

The Meaning of Authority

27. *Authority and community cannot be separated from each other any more than a human body can be separated from its skeleton. As there is no body without a bone structure, so there is no community without structures. That is: to be a community has its own demands.*

One purpose of this thesis is to discard forcefully a false approach to authority in community; another is to give a succinct but substantial explanation of how authority arises and operates in a community.

We need to discard a false approach as it opposes authority in community as if they were two disparate entities. It can manifest itself through an unduly sharp distinction between superiors and subjects, a terminology that Vatican Council II tried to avoid. It sometimes camouflages itself by stressing the difference between "the leaders" and "those who are led," a language certainly not borrowed from the Bible. Verbal expressions, insignificant as they may look, shape the mind, and the mind creates practical attitudes.

In a healthy community, the two are organically united; one cannot exist without the other. Authority is the central organ of the community; its task is to create and to maintain unity in the group. Communal authority has no external source; it is a necessary creation from the inside. Nor is it opposed to the community: it is an integral part of it. Let us explain further.

To have a multitude of persons together at the same place and in the same time is not enough to form a community. There are thousands of persons at Grand Central Station in New York City around five o'clock in the afternoon; yet, who would claim that they are forming a community? They are not, because no bond of unity holds them together. If anything, they are rushing away from each other trying to catch their trains. A multitude of persons becomes a community when they are inspired by the same ideas and when they act for the same purpose.

Such unity in a group does not fall from heaven. The group must create it.

To promote common vision and action is precisely the essence of authority. Its capacity to pull and hold the whole body together comes from power. It may be power given by the Spirit of God; it may be power that comes from human intelligence and determination; it may be power given legally by a larger community, of which a smaller one is part. Authority, however, is rooted in power.

We should not be afraid of the word "power." True, in modern English it may imply naked and brutal force, but its ancient Christian meaning is quite different; power means the strength of the Spirit in a human being. Such power is the foundation of all authority in the Church. This is nowhere better expressed than in *Lumen Gentium*, where the council tried to explicate the deeper meaning of the authority of the pope and the bishops:

> The Roman Pontiff, as the successor of Peter, is the perpetual and visible source and foundation of the unity both of the bishops and of the whole company of the faithful. Individual bishops are the visible source and foundation of unity in their own particular churches, which are modelled on the universal church. (23)

Further, since authority is the bond of unity, it cannot function unless accepted by those who are under it or around it. Permanent and free dedication to the community on both sides holds the body together.

The interplay between the central organ of the body and the rest of it—that is, between those members of the community who are vested with power and authority and those who are not—is an ongoing interaction of vital forces. Those in authority cannot operate unless they have the capacity and willingness to receive a multitude of ideas or suggestions, from all they claim to direct. If no such receptivity exists, authority ceases to be a living organ in the body; after all, how can the head function if it does not receive blood and oxygen from the body?

Having received the suggestions, those in authority must play their specific and crucial role. They must create and sustain a common vision and a common goal out of the multiplicity of ideas and purposes. It is necessary to listen to all; otherwise, the process of governing cannot even begin. The task of authority does not end there: it must help all to find a new unity.

Therefore, those in authority ought to communicate the new vision to all the members. They should not impose the vision on the community but communicate it to them in such a way that they can understand and accept it out of their internal freedom. It is in only this way that the community becomes of one mind and of one heart.

So much explains the birth and the life of a community through the creative action of a center, or the birth of authority through the creative action of the community. If a loose group wants to become a community, it must generate authority.

In the Church, there is a transcendental source of unity: the Word of God guiding everyone and the energizing Spirit alive in each person draw the members together. The Word and the Spirit are one source of life for all; they are the ultimate rule and measure of all actions of the head and of the members.

This relationship created by the Word and the Spirit distinguishes the ecclesial community from secular associations. In a democratic system of civil government the will of the people, manifested through the usual procedures of voting and electing, can be, indeed, in ordinary circumstances it must be, the norm of action for the government. In an ecclesial community, the will of the people, no less than the will of those in government, is subject to the exacting demands of the Word and of the Spirit.

The Right Use of Authority

28. *Authority vested in a person is a sacred trust. Even when its legal limitations are few, its use is subject to moral and religious norms. Authority in an ecclesial community must be used for the sake of God's Kingdom only.*

The center of power exists for the sake of the whole body; to exercise authority is one of the ministries in the community. Not one ounce of power and might is given for the exaltation of the center; it is entirely ordered and destined for the building and strengthening of the whole body.

To achieve their mandate, those in authority must have an absolute respect for objective values. Therefore, if they discover a gift in the community, for example, an exceptional talent for music in one of the members, the right question for them is, "How can this gift be inserted into the operation of the whole group?" It does not mean that the whole should adjust to this one talent, but it means that we must not lightly sacrifice an individual and his or her talent to an abstract common goal. Admittedly, to strike the right balance that respects both the good of the individual and the common good may not always be easy.

The attitude of those in authority will be very different if they look at a gift in the community as if it were their own property, therefore freely disposable, or if they look at it as a sacred trust that brings with it the burden of fair accounting.

Models of Authority

29. *Although our understanding of authority underwent serious changes in modern times, such changes did not destroy what was good in the old conception but corrected and perfected it.*

The reasons for changes are manifold. The world has become much more sophisticated. The standards of education are more rigorous, and many communities have become associations of highly trained and specialized persons. The model of father-son or mother-daughter relationship are no longer applicable.

While to be in authority remains a distinct ministry, an indispensable one at that, it is no longer correct to assume that the superior is the best-informed and most intelligent person, as a parent is for a child. He is as limited as the others are. Yet even in present-day communities, a center of unity is necessary. If we must build it on a model, the most suitable one is that of a "trusted friend" endowed with power to serve his or her people. Communities should no longer be looked on as groups of children directed by a father or a mother, but as groups of friends who want one of them endowed with power to hold them together in faith, hope, and love and thereby make their work more effective. The operation of authority described earlier is not possible if we follow the parent-child model; after all, there cannot be a steady and fair exchange of advice between parents and children. Something is wrong when mature adults pretend that some of them are children. They are all children in relationship to God, adults in relationship to each other.

Internal Inspiration—External Government

30. *In ordinary government, it is wise—nay, imperative—to honor the distinction and keep the distance between the internal forum and the external forum. Prophecy and administration are two distinct ministries. They should not be confused—not in theory and not in practice.*

Internal forum means the internal domain reserved to God and to a person alone—and rightly so. External forum means the field where the ordinary power to govern operates in a community.

The vision and inspiration of a person rule his or her conscience. Laws and precepts organize and direct the external life of the community. We should not consider the two fields as opposed. Rather, they should complete each other and together, by cooperating, they should bring peaceful and purposeful times to the community.

Internal judgments and deliberations are concerned with the world of conscience. Government is about coordination of activities and establishing norms that help to build the best attainable harmony between the welfare of individual persons and the common good of all. The strength of a conscientious decision comes from the internal resources of a person; the power to govern comes from a mandate given by the community, either through elections or by appointment.

A community is prosperous when there is respect for both conscience and government, when each of the two functions according to its own purpose without supplanting or canceling out the other. Neither of the two should be weakened; they should grow strong together.

Day-by-Day Government

31. *While community discernment can serve an important purpose when the community is reaching crossroads, it is hardly suitable for ordinary governance.*

In the history of every community, there are times when the community has come to crossroads and must make important decisions. Those are times for prayerful deliberation. The Hebrews had to stop to reflect and to pray after they escaped from Egypt and before they began to turn toward the Promised Land. They had an ideal setting for discernment: the desert of Sinai with God's mountain in the background!

Yet, the great and valuable spiritual instrument of communal discernment is not for deciding everyday issues, trends, or currents. It is not for trivialities.

Indeed, historically the somewhat solemn procedure of discernment never functioned for long as an instrument of ordinary everyday government. If it existed, after a short while it gave way to an orderly decision-making process through discussions, deliberations, and counting the votes. The informal procedure of the Council of Jerusalem developed into formal structures in later councils until at Vatican II computers were brought in to count the votes and thus to help to assess the movement of the Spirit with speed and accuracy. Nothing is wrong with giving a spiritual purpose to a machine built with human intelligence!

In the history of religious communities, a similar evolution has taken place. The early simplicity of the brethren, whether they were monks, mendicant friars, or regular priests, developed into a structured type of government such as chapters, congresses, or congregations that work according to well-defined rules. The law of evolution is that structure follows enthusiasm. Institutions give historical stability to fragile inspirations.

Each community should have the wisdom to know in what circumstances it should turn to discernment. A precious instrument can be destroyed when used at the wrong place in the wrong time; yet, precious values can be lost if a good instrument is not used at the right place in the right time.

Fifth Question

What Practical Guidelines Follow from Our Theological Reflections?

The following practical guidelines do not contain new insights. They sum up practical attitudes and actions for communities intent on discernment.

1. A community intent on discernment should recall the words of the Lord: "For which of you, intending to build a tower, does not first sit down and estimate the cost, to see whether he has enough to complete it?" (Luke 14:28). Its first resolve should be to keep the height and width of the tower proportionate to its gifts of nature and grace.

2. A community should not literally imitate any historical model of discernment unless the members' own circumstances are identical or very similar to that model and their own resources are as abundant as those whom they follow. Since the first fathers of the Society of Jesus were a small and deeply contemplative community, formed and trained by Ignatius for many years, and since they deliberated over an exceptional religious issue to which only a grace-filled inspiration could

give a reliable answer, their method and resources were unique. Consequently, the model needs adjusting before other communities begin to use it in radically different circumstances.

3. Although an ordinary community concerned with lesser issues may not be able to operate with such deep insights and such firm design as the first Jesuits did, its members should be able to seek and find the next step in the service of the Lord. Therefore, they should not be afraid to use community discernment whenever they must face important decisions.

4. The Lord blesses communities in different ways. The issues they face are different too. Hence, adjustments in the method of finding the next step in the service of the Lord are always necessary. No pattern is universal.

5. Peace is a fundamental condition for successful discernment in all communities. If there is no peace in the community, a search for reconciliation should be the only object of discernment.

6. The more a community is susceptible to the vagaries of emotional instability, the less it is disposed for genuine discernment.

7. To expect an answer from the Father (as Jesus promised) is right when putting the question in the name of the Lord Jesus and in the Spirit, but no one should tempt God by raising a question out of his or her own resources and then postulating an answer by a fixed date. The Scriptures abundantly condemn such presumption. The community should know how to wait patiently when God alone can give the answer. Remember that no human effort can hasten Christ's intervention. Our impatience could easily lock us into a false solution.

8. When the community has the capacity to resolve a problem by using its members' own resources of grace and nature, it should not expect a revelation, but it should go ahead to find the best solution it can. The fundamental rule for any method is that all the exchanges and deliberations should be soaked in prayer.

9. The community can make good progress by focusing in prayer and reflection on each side of an issue, especially when the answer to a question must be a *yes* or a *no.* This was the method of the first Jesuits; it suited their purpose perfectly. It may suit the purpose of some latter-day communities as well, but the method is not exclusive of other procedures.

10. When the question does not allow a simple *yes* or *no* answer, communities must work out other methods that allow for steady, ongoing contributions from many sources. We must use different working methods for deciding the questions, "Should we build a tower?" and "How should we build it?" This distinction is particularly relevant for communities that are intent on writing constitutional documents.

11. While all should make an effort to understand and judge every point of view, all should respect also the one-sidedness of a prophet and the penetrating but circumscribed insights of a genius. Historically, there are many times when a unique inspiration from God or an unusual insight into nature made a prophet or a genius unreceptive to arguments that seemed good to everybody else. The community should treasure such persons. They make up in depth what they lack in breadth.

12. Throughout the process of communal discernment, each member should participate wholeheartedly, both in giv-

ing and in receiving. If someone fails in either way, the whole body suffers.

13. Peace, consolation, and encouragement are signs of God's grace and presence. They confirm the conscience of the community that is intent on taking the next step in the Lord's service. We can consider the objective value of such a step in two ways. First, in relation to the community: it may be the best for them because it is the most they can do. Second, in relation to other communities, including the universal Church and our human society: it may be good or bad; it may bring progress or disaster. An incompetent child can do his very best in driving a train and still cause it to derail and involve many others in the disaster. A competent person drives it properly and ensures peace for all. This rule remains valid and is compatible with the belief that the presence of the Risen Lord enhances the capacity of the community to serve him.

14. The community should be cautious and remain realistic in its aim. It should not try to create a *Utopia* here and now. When someone holds no responsibility for the practical execution of the decision, it is easy to be fascinated and carried away by perfection. Yet, what is perfect in the abstract can become destructive in the concrete order. The best can be the enemy of the good.

15. Community discernment should be an ongoing process. The actual time of discernment is no more than an intense period in the continuously evolving life of the community. Discernment must blend into a broader movement of life.

16. Community discernment must be a self-correcting process. When the community articulates what the next step

is, there is a fallible human element in its judgment. It is subject to correction. Since our sinful condition makes our vision blurred, our insights limited, our decisions less than the best, we must continually examine and reexamine what we have been doing.

17. There should be room for dissent in community discernment. Indeed, dissent should be welcome and manifest for all to see. The dissenting voices of today are often the beginning of a new dawn for tomorrow. None should pressure another into a common opinion. God loves persons in a community.

18. After the conclusion of the process of community discernment, it is wise to evaluate it. As an individual should reflect on his or her own thoughts and actions, so should a community. The whole community should not perform the evaluation, but a small group of trusted and qualified persons who have taken part in the process or were present throughout it. They should then report to the community.

To avoid any prejudice or bias, they should ask a number of objective questions. Here are some examples:

- Was every member of the discerning community thoroughly acquainted with all the relevant facts?
- Were they sufficiently learned and versed in the subject matter of the discernment?
- Were they given ample time for reflection and for developing original insights, or did they labor under pressure?
- Were the participants peaceful, quiet, and receptive?

- Was the climate prayerful?
- What role did critical intelligence play?

True answers to questions such as these may reveal more of the value of discernment than a diffused feeling of peace and happiness. Furthermore, a community may want to follow the rule that it will not enter a new discernment process until they have objectively evaluated the last one.

19. Community discernment can be a powerful instrument of progress in the life of a religious community, provided we do not expect wonders and miracles from it. It can assure quiet growth in grace and wisdom.

In Place of Conclusion

The conclusion to any study may have two dimensions. One emerges from looking back on the field covered by the author: a summing up of the questions and answers that succeeded each other in the process of reflection. Another springs from a look forward beyond the field just explored.

The practical guidelines that we gave in the last part of this essay sum up sufficiently the gist of our questions and answers; there is no need to recall them again. Yet, we believe there is a need to point beyond the scope of this study, even beyond all the benefits and blessings that communal discernment can bring. In doing so, we take our inspiration from St. Paul. He wrote in his first epistle to the Corinthians:

> Now there are varieties of gifts, but the same Spirit; and there are varieties of services, but the same Lord; and there are varieties of activities, but it is the same God who activates all of them in everyone. To each is given the manifestation of the Spirit for the common good. (1 Cor 12:4-7)

All the gifts must be used for the common good, that is, for the good of the whole body that is the Church. The gift of discernment too, when granted to a community, is given for the sake of a larger and more universal body than the discerning community itself. Indeed, a religious group reflecting about the next step they will take in the service of the Lord can do so validly only when they look beyond themselves and their main goal is to build and to strengthen the whole body that is the Church. Love and compassion for the Church of Christ is always the sign of the presence of his Spirit, just as the lack of those attitudes is a virtually infallible sign of the absence of the Spirit of Christ.

The gift of discernment, however, is not the highest gift:

> And I will show you a still more excellent way. If I speak in the tongues of mortals and of angels, but do not have love, I am a noisy gong or a clanging cymbal. And if I have prophetic powers, and understand all mysteries and all knowledge, and if I have all faith, so as to remove mountains, but do not have love, I am nothing. (1 Cor 12:31–13:2)

Would Paul write today: "If I have the capacity to discern in all matters of heaven and earth, but do not have love, I am nothing"?

All discerners should aim for the more excellent way: "And now faith, hope, and love abide, these three; and the greatest of these is love" (1 Cor 13:13).

Further Readings

The purpose of this list of books is "inspirational," that is, to lead the reader into broader horizons concerning the theological roots and the history of discernment.

Augustine, Bishop of Hippo. *Confessions.*

The immortal story of a young man discerning his vocation.

Benedict, St., Abbot. *The Rule of St. Benedict in English.* Edited by Timothy Fry. Collegeville, MN: Liturgical Press, 2018.

"This is advice from a father who loves you; welcome it and faithfully put it into practice." From the Prologue by Benedict, who was and remains truly the Master of discretion and discernment.

Guillet, Jacques, and others. "Discernement des esprits." In *Dictionnaire de Spiritualité: Ascétique et mystique, doctrine et histoire.* Vol. 3, 1222–91. Paris: Beauchesne, 1957.

A full theological treatise on discernment covering every aspect: biblical, historical, and systematic.

Haggerty, Donald. *Contemplative Enigmas: Insights and Aid on the Path to Deeper Prayer*. San Francisco: Ignatius Press, 2020.

A secure and sound guide for discernment in contemplative prayer.

Heschel, Abraham J. *The Prophets.* New York: Harper Collins, 2001.

The mandate of the prophets was to discern the movements of God's Spirit in the world. Heschel's book contains much about how they fulfilled their mission. Much of what they said and how they said it contains lessons for our times; see in particular the chapter "Theology of Pathos." Highly recommended.

Ignacio de Loyola. *Obras Completas.* Edited by Ignacio Iparraguirre and Candido de Dalmases. Biblioteca de Autores Cristianos. Madrid: La Editorial Catolica, 1963.

The original Ignatian sources in a one-volume edition with numerous concise notes and references.

Ivens, Michael. *Understanding the Spiritual Exercises.* Leominster, England: Gracewing, 1998.

An outstanding commentary on the Exercises by a learned and insightful person.

Kiser, John. *The Monks of Tibhirine: Faith, Love, and Terror in Algeria.* New York: St. Martin's Press, 2002.

Community discernment; martyrdom was the issue.

Newman, John Henry. *An Essay on the Development of Christian Doctrine.* Garden City, NY: Doubleday, 1960.

O'Malley, John W. *The First Jesuits.* Cambridge, MA: Harvard University Press, 1993.

How a handful of wise men created and consolidated the Society of Jesus through ongoing informal and formal discernments.

Pegon, Joseph, and Raymond Studzinski. "Discernment, Spiritual." *New Catholic Encyclopedia.* 2nd ed. Vol. 4, 765–67. Washington, DC: Catholic University of America, 2003.

Summary article; essential bibliography.

Servais, Jacques, ed. *Hans Urs von Balthasar on the Ignatian Spiritual Exercises: An Anthology.* Translated from the German by Thomas Jacobi and Jonas Wernet. San Francisco: Ignatius Press, 2019.

A book rich in insightful reflections about discernment.

Therrien, Gerard. *Le discernement dans les écrits pauliniens.* Etudes Bibliques. Paris: Gabalda, 1973.

A scholarly work with ample bibliography.

Vries, Piet Penning de. *Discernment of Spirits.* Translated from the Dutch by W. Dudok Van Heel. New York: Exposition Press, 1973. *An introduction into the doctrine of St. Ignatius of Loyola on discernment based on original sources.*